Coca-Cola

ASSOULINE

TIME

THE WEEKLY NEWSMAGAZINE

FOREWORD

In this, our 125th-anniversary year, we wanted to do something special to honor everyone who has "paused and refreshed" with a Coca-Cola for the past century and a quarter.

This book is our way of saying thank-you to our consumers around the world who, within just the next twenty-four hours, will once again reach for more than 1.6 billion servings of ice-cold Coca-Cola beverages.

This is not a book of commercials. We did not commission many of the images you see here. The photos and icons and art on these pages capture the way Coca-Cola is owned by the people who enjoy it.

If there's one thing I have learned while working for our wonderful Coca-Cola system during the last thirty-two years, it is that enjoying a Coca-Cola is a simple pleasure that everyone relates to—world leaders, movie stars, famous athletes, you, and me. It's a shared experience, a common thread that ties our diverse world together. Andy Warhol once wrote, "You can be watching TV and see Coca-Cola, and you can know that the president drinks Coke, Liz Taylor drinks Coke, and just think, you can drink Coke, too."

As Coca-Cola employees, we were taught early on that we are mere stewards of our brands. Ownership resides with those who entrust us to provide them with affordable, high-quality, great-tasting, and unparalleled refreshment.

In 1950, when *Time* wanted to recognize Coca-Cola, the magazine asked then–company president Robert Woodruff to grace its cover.

He refused, insisting that Coca-Cola wasn't about any man but rather about the brand. As a result, one of the most iconic magazine covers of all time was born—and you see it here in this book: Coca-Cola literally put its arms around a thirsty world in an embrace, offering it up a taste of ice-cold refreshment.

The photos, illustrations, and other images in this book tell the story of history, technology, pop culture, and the march of commerce during the last 125 years.

Since May 8, 1886, when Dr. John Pemberton sold the first Coca-Cola for a nickel in Jacob's Pharmacy in Atlanta, Coca-Cola has grown exponentially. From that warm, sunny day in Georgia onward, Coca-Cola has gone on to connect with more people in more places than any other product the world has ever known. In fact, Coca-Cola has become the world's most recognized brand.

While our tradition of consumer engagement continues today through new technologies and channels like social media, the underlying message remains timeless: From the point of thirst to the point of consumption, our consumers look to us to share their values.

Throughout my career, I have had the privilege of experiencing our consumers embracing not only our beverages but also the ideals we represent. Whether it is in a remote outpost of western China or on the bustling streets of New York, New Delhi, or Nairobi, you sense a yearning among people for happiness, friendship, family, and opportunity.

In these places and in so many others, you sense the optimism, the belief that a better day is coming—not just a better business day, but a better day for humanity. Coca-Cola has always represented that optimism, the magical force that underscores and celebrates our humanity.

That's truly our secret formula.

All of the images in this book have sprung from the strength of a great product and a great brand. But they also took enormous effort, and I want to recognize the creative energies behind each of them. Today, thanks to the dedication and the vision of our more than three hundred bottling partners and the twenty million retail customers who sell our beverages, Coca-Cola anchors a portfolio of more than five hundred brands and more than 3,300 beverages that are found in 206 countries.

Our company and bottling partners around the world today stand on the broad shoulders of the countless pioneers and visionaries and hardworking employees who believed in Coca-Cola and its promise.

If you haven't done so already, find a comfortable place to read, grab yourself an ice-cold Coca-Cola, and then sit back and enjoy.

Muhtar Kent
Chairman of the Board, Chief Executive Officer
The Coca-Cola Company

" What's great about this country is that America started the tradition where the richest consumers buy essentially the same things as the poorest. You can be watching TV and see Coca-Cola, and you know that the President drinks Coke, Liz Taylor drinks Coke, and just think, you can drink Coke, too. A Coke is a Coke and no amount of money can get you a better Coke than the one the bum on the corner is drinking. All the Cokes are the same and all the Cokes are good. Liz Taylor knows it, the President knows it, the bum knows it, and you know it. "

ANDY WARHOL
THE PHILOSOPHY OF ANDY WARHOL (FROM A TO B AND BACK AGAIN)

A sign of good taste.

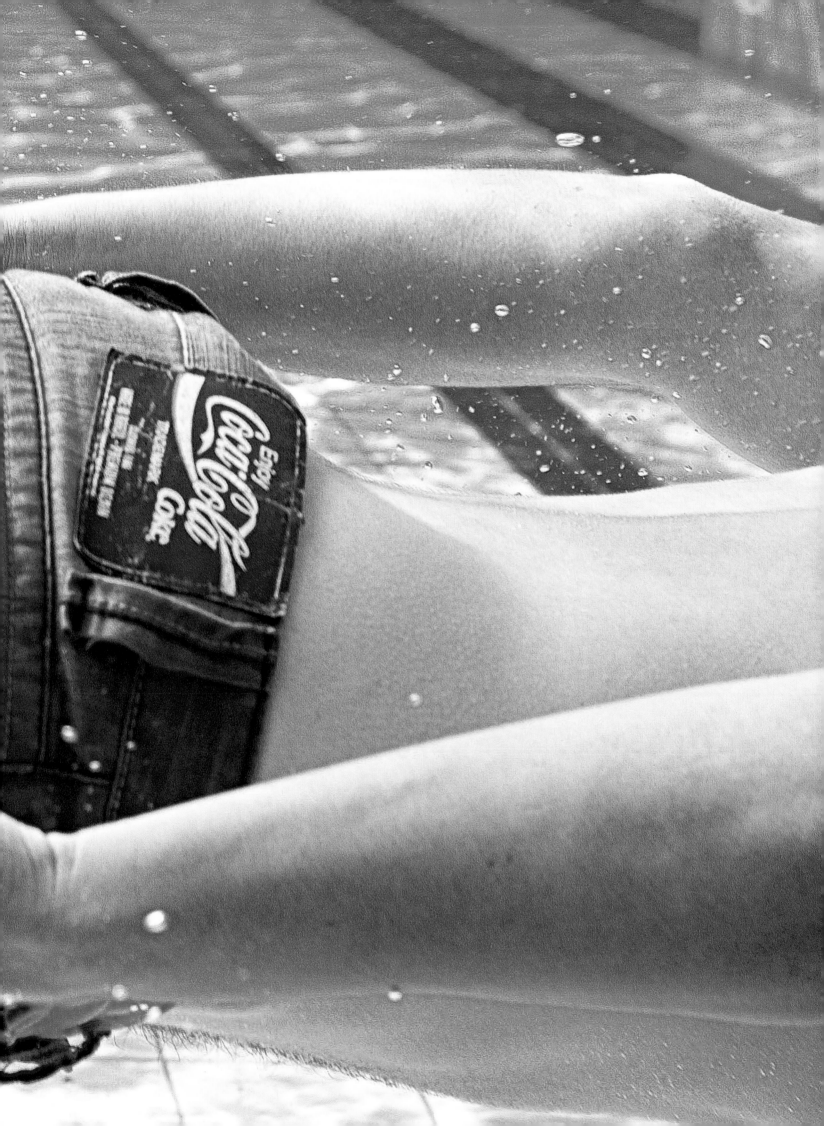

"Travel where you will, anywhere in the world, and you will encounter Coca-Cola on clothes, in signs, on packaging, in art everywhere."

JUDITH EVANS
REDESIGNING IDENTITY

"It was a nice breakfast—two hard boiled eggs, a piece of Danish, and a Coca-Cola spiked with gin."

JOHN CHEEVER
THE CHIMERA

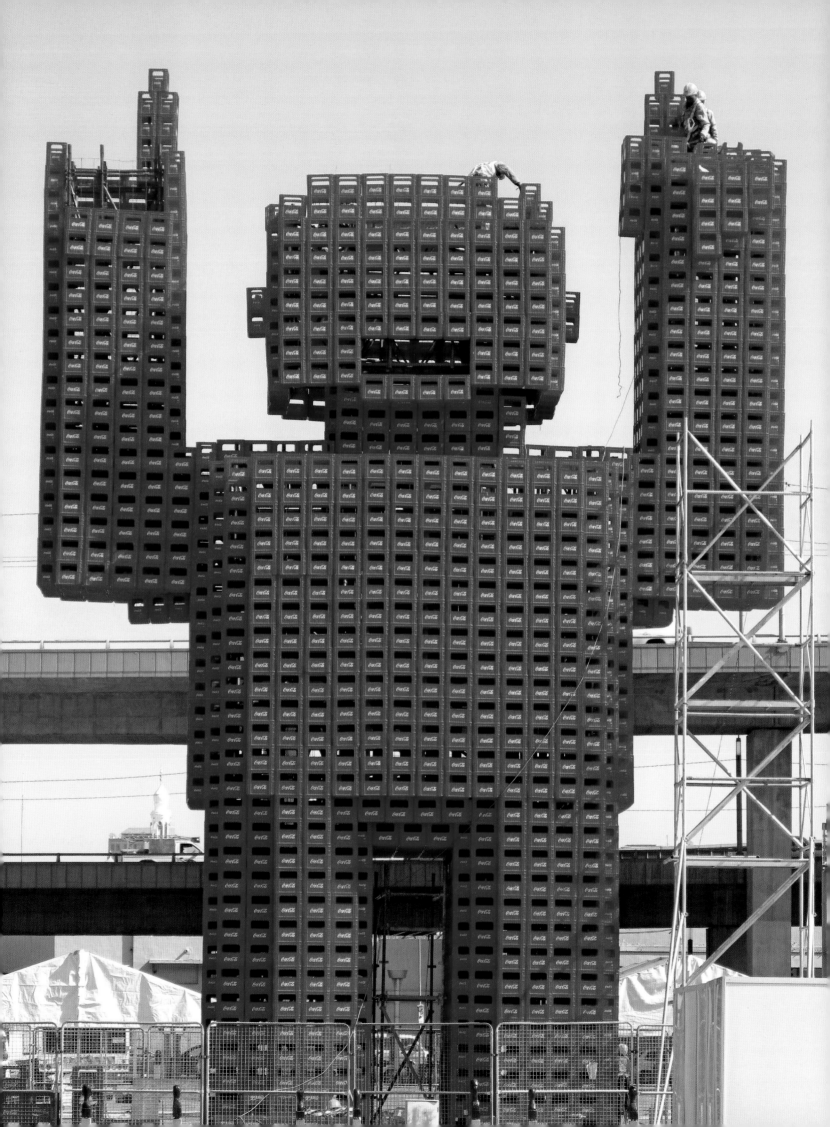

"I met her in a club down in old Soho where you drink champagne and it tastes just like Coca-Cola, C-O-L-A cola."

RAY DAVIES (THE KINKS)
LOLA

Coca-Cola A Bottle of Hope.

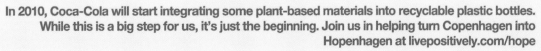
In 2010, Coca-Cola will start integrating some plant-based materials into recyclable plastic bottles. While this is a big step for us, it's just the beginning. Join us in helping turn Copenhagen into Hopenhagen at livepositively.com/hope

"Americans wanted to settle all our difficulties with Russia and then go to the movies and drink Coke."

WILLIAM AVERELL HARRIMAN
FORMER POLITICIAN, BUSINESSMAN, AND DIPLOMAT

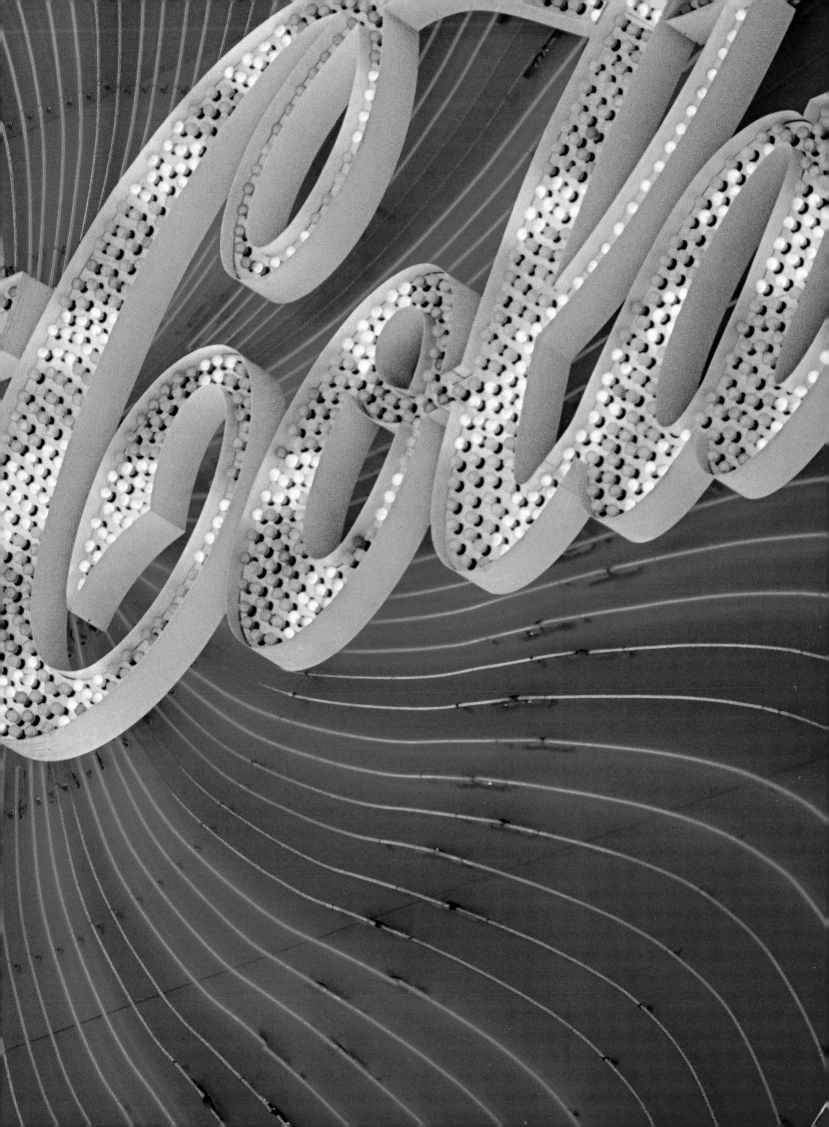

"Coca-Cola, the ultimate and enduring icon of refreshment."

NEVILLE ISDELL
FORMER CEO, THE COCA-COLA COMPANY, 2007

"There are things in American culture that want to wipe the class distinction. Blue jeans. Ready-made clothes. Coca-Cola."

Leslie Fiedler
Literary critic

"Without a Coca-Cola life is unthinkable."

HENRY MILLER
The Air-Conditioned Nightmare

"The Cokes are in the icebox, the popcorn's on the table."

SAM COOKE
HAVING A PARTY

"A billion hours ago, human life appeared on Earth.
A billion seconds ago, the Beatles changed music forever.
A billion Coca-Colas ago, was yesterday morning."

Roberto Goizueta
Former CEO, The Coca-Cola Company, 1996

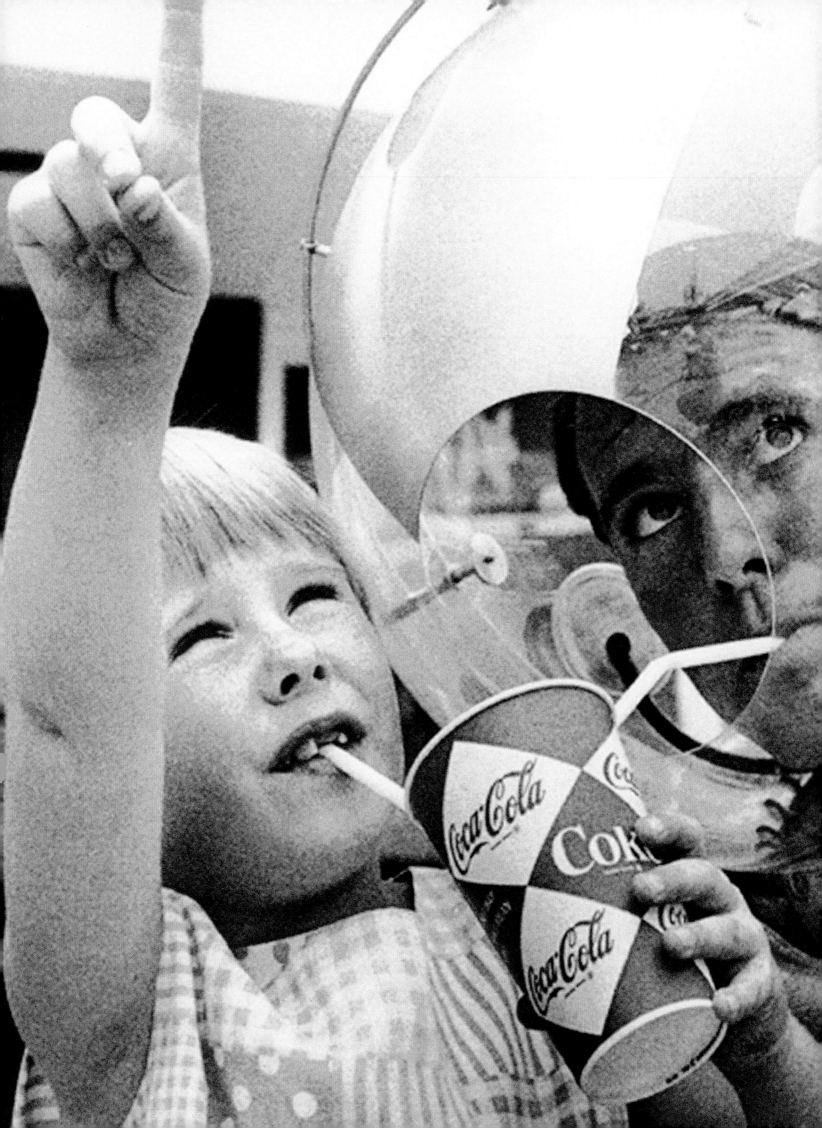

"Drinkin' rum and Coca-Cola
Go down Point Koomahnah
Both mother and daughter
Workin' for the Yankee dollar."

ANDREWS SISTERS
RUM AND COCA-COLA

Refreshes you best.

GOOD

PAUSE

DR...
Coca-...
IN B...

Join t

DRINK

Coca-Co

TRADE-MARK ®

IN BOTTL

...he friendly circle

Have a Coke
and a Smile.

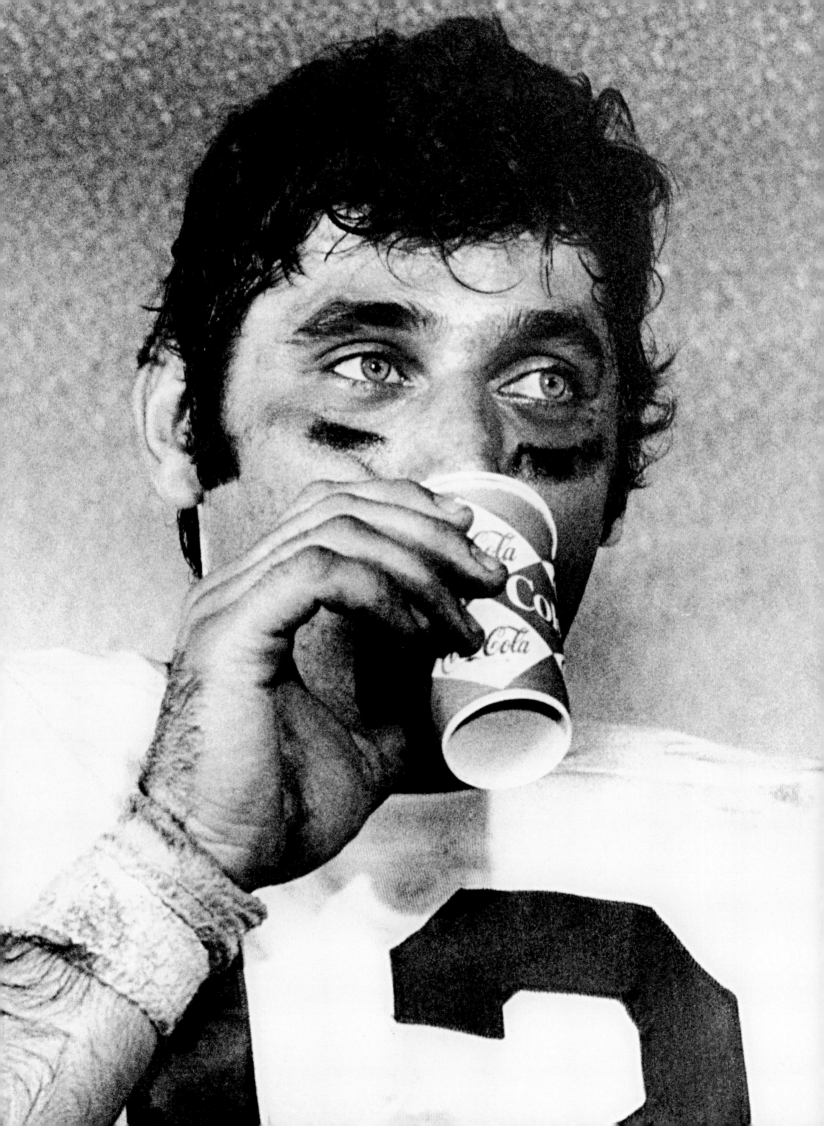

Take Home Plenty of Coke

"Coca-Cola is not just a product. It is much more than that to the consumers of this country. Coca-Cola is a part of people's lives."

Donald R. Keough
Former President, The Coca-Cola Company, 1987

y

es

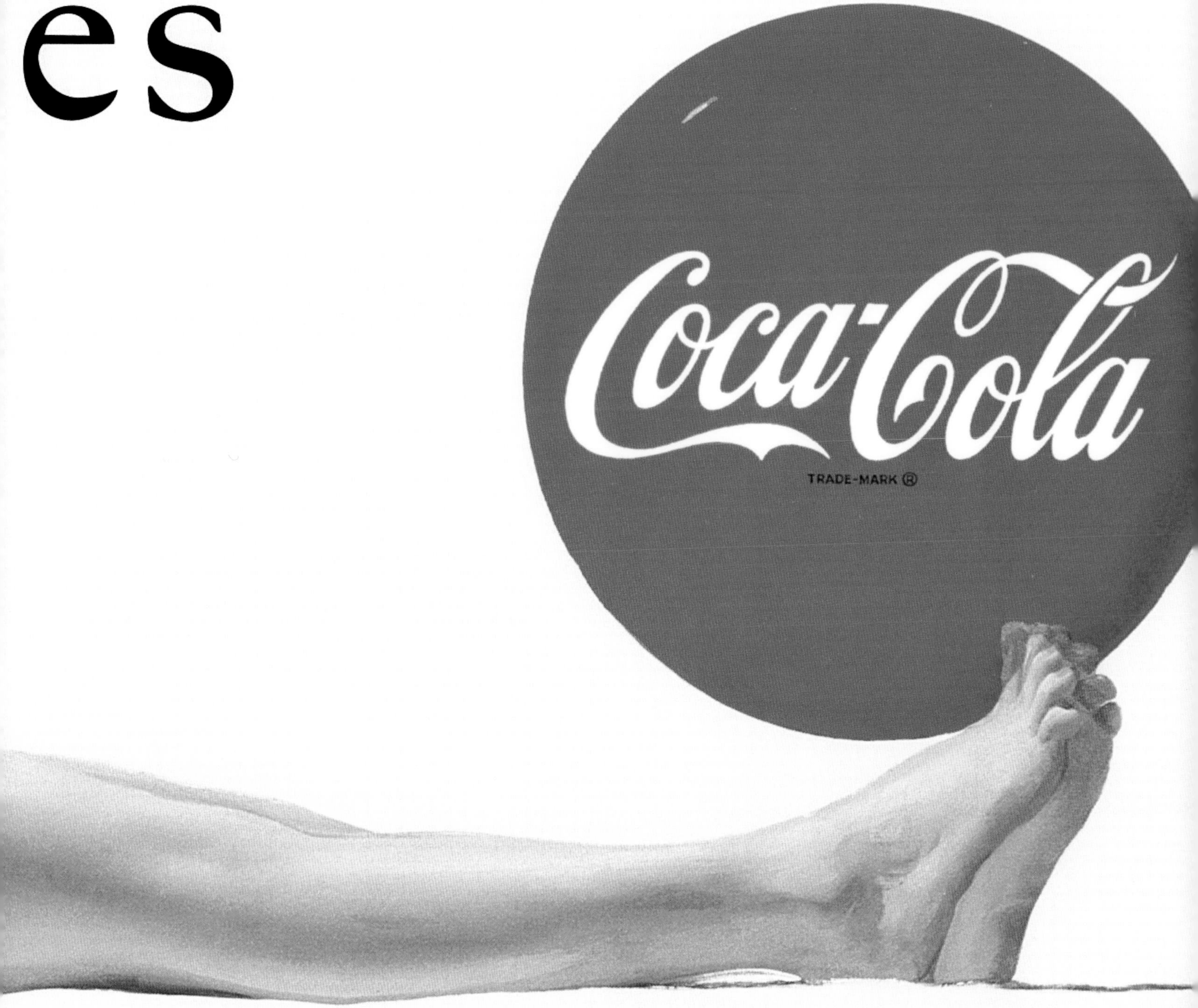

"Coca-Cola should always be within an arm's reach of desire."

ROBERT W. WOODRUFF
FORMER CHAIRMAN, THE COCA-COLA COMPANY, 1923

Travel refreshed

"Love is two people sipping Coca-Cola from the same straw on a warm sunny day."

LAMAR COLE
POET

Coca-Cola goes along.

Delicious and
refreshing.

"The fact that we are a thriving business nearly 125 years later is a testament to our youth, not our age."

Muhtar Kent
Chairman and CEO, The Coca-Cola Company, 2011

BUVEZ

Coca-Cola

TRADE MARK

Coca-Cola was the first commercial product to appear on the cover of *Time*. The magazine originally wanted longtime company leader Robert W. Woodruff's image on the cover, but he refused, saying the brand Coca-Cola itself should be featured, 1950.

Pop art by Sir Peter Blake commissioned by Coca-Cola UK, 2008.

The "Fairytale in a Vending Machine" advertisement from the Coca-Cola Happiness Factory series was a winner of the Cannes Silver Lion award, 2006.

A television advertisement that takes viewers on a magical journey through a Coca-Cola vending machine into a fantasy world known as the Coca-Cola Happiness Factory, 2007.

A group of colorful insects band together to perform an elaborate heist of a Coca-Cola bottle from a napping picnicker in this television advertisement, 2010.

A pop art Coca-Cola bottle advertisement from Sydney, Australia, 1998.

China, 2000.

Supermodel Naomi Campbell with Coca-Cola can rollers, shot by Ellen von Unwerth, 1991.

"Hard Times" features characters from *The Simpsons*, notably Mr. Burns, who learns to appreciate life's simple pleasures when faced with the loss of his fortune. First aired during Super Bowl XLIV, 2010.

Professional athlete Hidetoshi Nakata and Special Olympian Peter Okocha at the inaugural match of the "Unity Cup" presented by Coca-Cola, on the same pitch that just hours later hosted the 2010 FIFA World Cup™ match. Johannesburg, South Africa. Photograph by Richard Corman, March 19, 2010.

Coca-Cola Clothing fashion advertisement, Brazil, 2010.

"Open Happiness" global campaign, 2011.

A model sports an embellished Coca-Cola cap during London Fashion Week, spring/summer 2011.

In a landscape of aliases, the most meaningful peer connections happen face-to-face in the television spot "Avatar," 2009.

The Coca-Cola Corporate Pavilion at the World Exposition in Shanghai featured beverage innovations, the latest in sustainable packaging, and "Happiness Events," including celebrity performances and animation on a 50-foot Coca-Cola bottle composed of 3,000 light panels, 2010.

Repurposed Coca-Cola crates make public art in Johannesburg, South Africa, 2010.

The hero of this gritty video game has a change of heart after drinking a Coca-Cola, 2007.

Actress Julia Stiles with a Coca-Cola can in *Allure* magazine, photographed by Dewey Nicks, 1999.

Original painting featuring the iconic Coca-Cola bottle and logo, by artist Steve Penley, 2008.

A Beijing Olympic Games television spot featuring animated likenesses of LeBron James and Yao Ming, 2008.

Somali musician K'naan performed his anthem "Wavin' Flag" at the 2010 FIFA World Cup™ in Johannesburg, South Africa, 2010.

A Coca-Cola vending machine is transformed into a machine that dispenses doses of happiness in this award-winning spot, 2010.

"Coke Side of Life" advertisements, 2007.

A poster celebrating Hopenhagen, a movement empowering citizens to work together to combat climate change, which was launched at the United Nations Climate Change Conference in Copenhagen, 2009.

Coca-Cola Enterprises worked with its suppliers to create diesel-electric hybrid delivery trucks—vehicles that are 30% more fuel efficient and reduce overall emissions by 30%—in 2009.

Ryan Seacrest enjoying a Coca-Cola on location at Smashbox, West Hollywood, photographed by Gary Land, 2009.

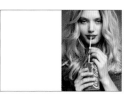

Model Bregje Heinen sipping Coca-Cola, photographed by Hunter & Gatti for Spanish fashion company Blanco's winter campaign, 2010.

In this television advertisement titled "It's Mine," Macy's Thanksgiving Day Parade balloons vie for a Coca-Cola bottle balloon in the skies of New York City, 2008.

Roger Milla, the legendary footballer from Cameroon, famed for his iconic celebratory dance during FIFA World Cup Italia™ on June 18, 1990, was featured in a Global TV ad during the FIFA World Cup 2010.

An animated bird celebrates the opening of Beijing's Bird's Nest stadium in a television spot, 2008.

An authentic reproduction of the original 1930s sign was installed in downtown in Atlanta, Georgia, in 2003.

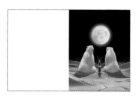

Polar bear advertisement inspired by the 1993 "Always Coca-Cola" campaign, 2002.

A member of the Coca-Cola pep squad in Casablanca, Morocco, wearing custom-made happiness slippers, celebrates the FIFA World Cup Trophy Tour, 2010.

U.S. President Bill Clinton and Hillary Rodham Clinton at Moscow's Coca-Cola bottling plant, 1995.

Actors Molly Ringwald, Judd Nelson, and Emilio Estevez with Coca-Cola cans in a scene from *The Breakfast Club*, 1985.

Coca-Cola apparel, designed by Tommy Hilfiger, was a fashion staple of the 1980's.

Actor Bill Cosby as a spokesperson for the "Have a Coke and a Smile" campaign, 1980.

Actress Sigourney Weaver in a scene from the film *Eyewitness*, 1980.

An advertisement featuring the influential rap group Run DMC, 1988.

An advertisement from the "Coke Adds Life" campaign, 1976.

A Coca-Cola advertisement from Japan, 1978.

Print advertisement featuring Julius Erving, known as Dr. J, for the "Coke is It!" campaign, 1984.

The classic red Coke machine provides a stark contrast to actor Willem Dafoe, clad in black leather, on the set of *The Loveless*, 1982.

In *Provincetown, 1976*, a photograph by Joel Meyerowitz, a Coca-Cola sign lights up the nighttime sky in summer 1976.

Print advertisement for "It's the Real Thing" campaign, 1973.

President Richard Nixon enjoying a burger and a Coca-Cola, 1970.

The television spot, "I'd Like to Buy the World a Coke," featured a multicultural cast singing in perfect harmony on a hilltop in Italy, 1971.

World Heavyweight Boxing Champion Muhammad Ali drinking Coca-Cola at a diner counter in Miami Beach, 1971.

Actor Yul Brynner enjoys the "real thing" on a break in production for *The Ultimate Warrior*, 1974.

Coca-Cola printed a poster of R&B great James Brown, 1970.

An advertisement capturing the energy of youth, ca. 1970.

Celebrity daredevil Evel Knievel drinks a Coca-Cola on the set of *Viva Knievel*, 1977.

Legendary football player Joe Greene starred in an iconic advertisement for The Coca-Cola Company, 1979.

NASCAR race-car driver Bobby Allison and pit crew wearing Coca-Cola pants, 1970.

A "For the Real Times" print advertisement, 1974.

Pages from a Coca-Cola brand identity book titled "This is the 70s," created by Lippincott and Margulies.

Actress Raquel Welch modeling a seventies jewelry collection, 1970.

Actor Michael Douglas on the set of *Hail, Hero!* 1969.

Ice-cold refreshment at the LBJ Ranch, Texas, 1965.

Three Coke Bottles, by Andy Warhol, 1960.

A Coca-Cola billboard illuminates Times Square, New York City, 1966.

A "Things Go Better with Coke" advertisement, 1965.

Ladies at Lunch: "Ice-Cold Coke Refreshes You Best," 1962.

Cindy Birdsong, Diana Ross, and Mary Wilson of the Supremes, 1968

Photograph from a Ray Charles recording session for a Coca-Cola commercial titled "Improving on Soul," 1967.

Rolling Stones bassist Bill Wyman, London, 1964.

A space exhibit at the reopening of Tomorrowland, in Disneyland, 1967.

John F. Kennedy at the Big Brother Awards dinner at the Mayflower Hotel in Washington, D.C., 1961.

The sultry "Lady in Red" advertisement from Brazil, 1950.

Entertainer Sammy Davis, Jr., on the set of *Porgy and Bess*, 1959.

An original painting later used as an advertisement, 1959.

Pop-singing trio, the McGuire Sisters, were featured in several Coca-Cola advertisements and television spots, 1960.

A Coca-Cola advertisement by pin-up artist Gil Elvgren, 1954.

An advertisement from the campaigns "Coke Time" and "Join the Friendly Circle," 1955.

Actress Grace Kelly drinking Coca-Cola and actor John Ericson on the set of *Green Fire*, 1956.

Comedy duo Dean Martin and Jerry Lewis quenching their thirst with a bottle of Coca-Cola, 1955.

American politician Adlai Stevenson cools off with a Coca-Cola in the hot Egyptian sun, 1953.

A grinning Elvis Presley enjoying Coca-Cola, 1956.

Artwork created for collegiate football game programs, 1950.

Celebrity football quarterback Joe Namath in a television spot for Coca-Cola, 1969.

A panoramic painting of young couples enjoying the slopes, used in a Coca-Cola "Be Really Refreshed" advertisement, 1959.

Coca-Cola stays in step with the times in this Brazilian advertisement featuring young women in the workforce, 1959.

A postcard featuring a Coca-Cola billboard over Piccadilly Circus, London, 1954.

An American serviceman and an admiring beauty enjoy Coca-Cola at a party in England, 1942.

On the set of the "The Frank Sinatra Show," ca. 1957.

A painting by artist Jack Potter used in Coca-Cola's "Sign of Good Taste" advertising campaign, 1957.

A Coca-Cola salesman delivering his ice-cold cargo via ski lift, 1964.

A young Italian couple enjoying Coca-Cola, 1962.

"There's Always Good Company in the Good Taste of Coke," advertisement created from a painting by Bernie Fuchs, 1957.

The entrance of The Coca-Cola Bottling Company building, ca. 1950.

Coca-Cola iconic glass contour bottles on the belt of a bottling plant in Atlanta, Georgia.

"Yes Girl," created from artist Haddon Sundblom's award-winning painting, was widely used in advertising for Coca-Cola, 1946.

Spectators walking in the Olympic Village, Rome, Italy, 1960.

Painted by noted illustrator Hayden Hayden, this image of the glamorous Coca-Cola Calendar Girl appeared on posters and serving trays, 1936.

Soldier at Home, a painting of an American family happily reunited after World War II, by artist Haddon Sundblom, 1945.

A smiling President Dwight D. Eisenhower pouring a Coca-Cola, 1952.

American movie star and former competitive swimmer Esther Williams offers a bottle of Coca-Cola to a snowman on skis, Sun Valley, Idaho, 1951.

A holiday poster and advertisement of Coca-Cola Santa and Sprite Boy, by artist Haddon Sundblom, 1949.

Funnyman Groucho Marx and comic foil Margaret Dumont sipping Coca-Cola in *At the Circus*, 1939.

An advertising poster of a young couple on a beach, by illustrator Hayden Hayden, 1935.

An illustration featuring a cowboy in the hot desert sun, cooling off with a Coca-Cola, 1941.

Artist Haddon Sundblom used his own image for the iconic Coca-Cola Santa, 1950.

Out Fishin', the first of six paintings by popular American artist Norman Rockwell for Coca-Cola, debuted on the company calendar, 1935.

Main entrance to the Olympic Village in Helsinki, Finland, 1952. Coca-Cola is a Worldwide Partner of the Olympic Games.

Brazilian pole vaulter Hélcio Buch Silva drinking a Coca-Cola, Helsinki, Finland, 1952.

A model in fencing dress leans on a Raymond Loewy–designed Coca-Cola cooler, 1947.

An advertising poster of teenagers enjoying Coca-Cola at a party, 1951.

Two men at the beach, balancing the quintessential American lunch: Coca-Cola and hot dogs, 1946.

Coca-Cola Victorian beauty in a feathered hat and flowers, 1901.

An early twentieth-century advertisement depicting fashionable travelers socializing at a soda fountain, 1910.

This "Thirst Knows No Season" advertisement proved that ice-cold Coca-Cola was as refreshing in winter as in summer, 1922.

In this turn-of-the-century advertisement, a sophisticated couple at the theater drinks Coca-Cola from fountain glasses, 1906.

A workman operates a bottle-capping machine at a Coca-Cola plant in Junction City, Kansas, 1910.

A Coca-Cola magazine advertisement with ladies golfing, 1914.

Early depictions of 1920s-era flappers, toasting life with ice-cold Coca-Cola, were used on calendars and serving trays, 1924.

The first appearance of a polar bear in Coca-Cola advertising, 1922.

Argentina point of sale decal for use on Coca-Cola coolers and shop doors, 1940.

Coca-Cola six pack carrier, 1940.

1886

May 8: Coca-Cola is created by John S. Pemberton and served at Jacobs' Pharmacy in Atlanta, Georgia. Nine drinks a day are sold during this year.

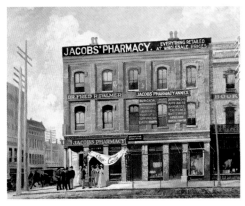

The Company's accountant, Frank Robinson, names the drink Coca-Cola, and thinking the two Cs would look well in advertising, pens the famous Spencerian script logo.

First newspaper advertisement appears using the slogans "Delicious and Refreshing" and "Drink Coca-Cola."

1887

The first coupons are used to promote Coca-Cola.

1891 First use of calendars for advertising by Asa Candler.

1892

Asa Candler, who had begun to acquire The Coca-Cola Company in 1888, finalizes the purchase and incorporates The Coca-Cola Company as a Georgia Corporation.

An annual advertising budget of $11,000 is authorized. The slogan, "A Delightful Summer or Winter Beverage" is launched.

1893

The trademark, Coca-Cola, having been in constant use since 1886, is registered with the U.S. Patent Office.

At the Company's second annual meeting, the first of an unbroken line of dividends is paid to investors.

1895 In the Company's annual report, Asa Candler declares that Coca-Cola is sold and drunk in every state and territory in the United States.

1896 First use of soda fountain urns and clocks for advertising purposes.

1898 First building erected for the sole purpose of housing The Coca-Cola Company. It was quickly outgrown as the Company moves to larger quarters five times in the next twelve years.

1899 The rights to bottle Coca-Cola in most of the United States are sold by Asa Candler to Benjamin F. Thomas and Joseph B. Whitehead of Chattanooga, Tennessee, for $1. Chattanooga became the first city to bottle Coca-Cola under the contract that year.

1901 The advertising budget surpasses
$100,000 for the first time.

1903 The first Coca-Cola Fountain Sales personnel convention
is held in Atlanta.

1904 The first advertising for Coca-Cola appears
in national magazines.

Annual sales of Coca-Cola hit the million-gallon mark.

1905 Lillian Nordica, an opera singer, and Hilda Clark,
a music hall performer, are the first celebrities to
endorse Coca-Cola.

Slogan: The Most Refreshing Drink in the World.
Slogan: Good All the Way Down.

1906 Bottling operations begin in Cuba, Panama,
and Canada, the first three countries outside the
United States to bottle Coca-Cola.

D'Arcy Advertising agency begins its 50-year association
with The Coca-Cola Company.

Straight-sided bottle first used in national advertising.

Slogan: The Ideal
Beverage for
Discriminating
People.

1907 The diamond-shaped paper label is trademarked.

The Company begins its long association with athletes with
a series of advertisements featuring noted baseball players.

Slogan: The Great National Drink at
the Great National Game.

Slogan: Good to the Last Drop.

1910 TOMESE
Coca-Cola
EN BOTELLITAS 6¢ PLATA

1911 The annual advertising budget for The Coca-Cola
Company surpasses $1 million for the first time.
The Company spends nearly $200,000 for painted
regional wall signs.

Slogan: Enjoy a Glass of Liquid Laughter.

1912 Bottling operations are started in the Philippines, the
Company's first expansion into Asia. The number of
bottlers in the United States rises to 691.

1913 Slogan: A Welcome Addition to Any Party.

1914 The calendar artwork for this year is named "Betty."
During this decade, two other named calendars appear,
"Elaine" and "Constance." These are the only instances
where models are named on calendars. Advertising also
appears on the back covers of pulp fiction novels.

Asa Candler makes a donation of one million dollars
to Emory University, beginning a long history of
philanthropy by Coca-Cola leadership.

1915 Answering the call of The
Coca-Cola Company and its
bottlers for a unique package,
the contour bottle is designed
by Alexander Samuelson and
patented by the Root Glass
Company. It is approved by
the Bottlers Association and
becomes the standard bottle
for Coca-Cola.

1917 The United States enters World War I, and sugar rationing
goes into effect, limiting the production of Coca-Cola.

Slogan: 3 Million a Day.

1919  The first bottling plants
are opened in Europe,
in Paris and Bordeaux.
The Coca-Cola Company
is purchased by a group
of investors lead by Ernest
Woodruff of the Trust
Company Bank for
$25 million. Coca-Cola
becomes a public stock
and is offered for $40
a share.

Slogan: Quality tells the difference.
Slogan: Whenever You See an Arrow, Think of Coca-Cola.

1920

Justice Oliver Wendell Holmes writes a Supreme Court decision ruling that Coca-Cola is a "single thing, from a single source and well known to the community," securing the trademark for the Company.

The Coca-Cola Company moves to its current location on North Avenue in Atlanta, Georgia.

First use of the slogan "Thirst Knows No Season" to help transition the product from a summer to a year-round beverage.

1923

Introduction of the first six-bottle carton, a significant innovation to the beverage industry. The carton is patented the following year.

Robert W. Woodruff is elected president of The Coca-Cola Company, beginning more than six decades of leadership in the business.

1925

The board of directors passes a resolution placing the secret formula for Coca-Cola in the bank vault at the Trust Company Bank in Atlanta, Georgia.

Outdoor billboards are introduced as part of the advertising mix.

1926

The Coca-Cola Foreign Department forms to supply syrup to overseas bottlers. Some of the countries where bottling operations begin during this decade include: Colombia, Belgium, Bermuda, China, Haiti, Italy, Germany, Holland, Spain, and Mexico.

1928

The Company begins its long-standing association with the Olympic Games by supplying Coca-Cola from kiosks surrounding the venues at the 1928 Amsterdam Games.

1929

The first large neon sign for Coca-Cola is placed in Times Square in New York City.

Slogan: The Pause That Refreshes.

Two significant innovations debut: The bell-shaped Coca-Cola fountain glass and the first standardized open-top cooler.

1930

The Coca-Cola Export Corporation is created to market Coca-Cola outside the United States.

1931

Seeking to create an advertising program that would link Coca-Cola with Christmas, artist Haddon Sundblom creates his first illustration showing Santa pausing for a Coca-Cola. For the next three decades, from 1931 to 1964, Sundblom paints images of Santa that influence the modern interpretation of St. Nick.

1932

Slogan: Ice Cold Sunshine.

1933

The first automated fountain dispenser, the Dole Master, is introduced at the Chicago World's Fair.

1935

Artist Norman Rockwell creates the 1935 *Out Fishin'* calendar. Rockwell also developed artwork for the 1931, 1932, and 1934 calendars.

Lettie Pate Evans joins the board of directors of The Coca-Cola Company. She is the first woman to serve on the board of a major corporation, a position she holds until 1953.

The first coin-operated vending machines are used by Coca-Cola.

1936

The fiftieth anniversary of Coca-Cola. Artist N. C. Wyeth creates the calendar for that year.

1938

Coca-Cola enters Australia, South Africa, Norway, and Austria.

Slogan: The Best Friend Thirst Ever Had.

1939

Robert W. Woodruff becomes Chairman of the Board. He serves until 1942. He later serves from 1952 to 1954. He was president of the company from 1923 to 1939.

Slogan: Coca-Cola Goes Along.

"Whoever You Are, Whatever You Do, Wherever You May Be, When You Think of Refreshment, Think of Coca-Cola."

1941
The United States enters World War II. Robert W. Woodruff orders that every man in uniform should get a bottle of Coca-Cola for 5 cents, wherever he is and whatever it costs.

The abbreviation "Coke" is used for the first time in magazine advertisements for Coca-Cola.

1942

The Sprite Boy character appears in magazine ads for the first time, affirming the use of "Coke."

1943
In the 1940s, women play a major role in the United States war effort and Coca-Cola recognizes them for doing so. The Company produces cardboard cutouts representing the majority of auxiliary women's units which were formed to assist in the war effort. Other advertising and promotional items, including bridge score pads, playing cards, calendars, and posters, show women in both military roles and at home. Women were also shown taking over some of the jobs at home that men traditionally held. Some of their positions are featured in the 1943 calendar and magazine advertisements as well.

1947

Industrial Designer Raymond Loewy's new sleek Coca-Cola fountain dispenser is introduced.

1950
Coca-Cola appears on the cover of *Time* magazine, and is the first commercial product to do so. The magazine originally wanted to place company leader Robert W. Woodruff's image on the cover, but he refused, saying the brand was the important thing and Coca-Cola itself should be featured.

First Coca-Cola TV advertisement airs.

1955
Family-size glass contour bottles are introduced in the United States, marking an important step in giving consumers packaging options to meet their needs. Until this point, Coca-Cola had been available only at the soda fountain and in 6½-ounce bottles.

Fanta Orange is introduced in Naples, Italy.

1959

The Arciform (also called the fishtail) logo is unveiled at bottlers' meetings.

1960   Coca-Cola in 12-ounce cans is introduced to the United States public, providing consumers with another package to meet their needs.

1961   Portfolio expands with introduction of Sprite.

1963   Tab is introduced as the first diet drink.

Slogan: Things Go Better with Coke.

1968

Special Olympics
Be a fan.

The Coca-Cola Company, which became a founding partner of Special Olympics when the organization was established in 1968 by Eunice Kennedy Shriver, has been deeply involved with both the summer and winter editions of the Special Olympics World Games.

1969   Slogan: # It's The Real Thing.

1970

The Dynamic Ribbon Device, often called the Coke "wave," is introduced to the public.

The 16-ounce can is introduced (steel-plated with aluminum lift-top end).

1971   First introduced as a radio advertisement and later produced as a television commercial, "I'd Like to Buy the World a Coke" becomes an international hit and remains one of the most popular ads for Coca-Cola.

1975   Georgia Coffee is introduced in Japan.

1976   Coca-Cola and FIFA (the Fédération Internationale de Football Association) agree to the first ever sponsorship between a company and an international sports governing body.

Slogan: Coke Adds Life.

1977   The contour bottle is granted registration as a trademark, a designation awarded to few other packages.

1978   Coca-Cola signs agreement to re-enter the China market after a nearly 30-year absence.

1979   The iconic Joe Greene television commercial debuts. The advertisement is consistently voted one of the best commercials of all time.

Slogan: Have a Coke and a Smile.

1981   Roberto C. Goizueta becomes chairman and CEO. He goes on to serve for 16 years in this role, and produces outstanding returns for the company's share owners. As a Cuban refugee who lived and relished the American dream, he said: "I came to this country with two possessions—my education and a job with The Coca-Cola Company."

1982   "Coke Is It!" advertising campaign is released.

Diet Coke is introduced, making soft drink history as the first extension of the trademarks Coca-Cola and Coke, and the most successful new soft drink since Coca-Cola itself. Within two years, Diet Coke becomes the top low-calorie soft drink in the world.

1985    After 99 years, a new formula for Coca-Cola (commonly called "new Coke") is introduced. The change startles the American public and leads to pundits calling it the "marketing blunder of the century," consumers hoarding the "old" Coke, and calls of protests by the thousands. The original formula returns 79 days later.

Coca-Cola becomes the first soft drink to be consumed in space when astronauts test the "Coca-Cola Space Can" aboard the space shuttle *Challenger*.

1986   Coca-Cola celebrates its centennial in Atlanta, Georgia, and announces the formation of the Coca-Cola Scholars Foundation.

1988   Slogan: Can't Beat the Feeling.

1989   Coca-Cola becomes the first trademark displayed in Pushkin Square, Moscow.

1991   First bottles made partially of recycled plastic, an innovation of the industry, are introduced.

1993   The Coca-Cola Polar Bear is introduced as part of the "Always Coca-Cola" campaign.

The 20-ounce plastic contour bottle is introduced.

1995   Coca-Cola travels into outer space for a third time, the first time with a woman: astronaut Eileen Collins.

1996   Atlanta, Georgia, is host for the Centennial Olympic Games. Today the site is home of the Georgia Aquarium and the new World of Coca-Cola.

2000   Coca-Cola announces a donation of 50 years of TV commercials to the Library of Congress in Washington, D.C.

The "Fridge Pack," a thinner, longer 12-pack carton for cans designed to take up less refrigerator space, is launched in the United States.

2004   A new 3-D, high-tech display in New York City's Times Square is illuminated. It is an advertising innovation more than six stories high.

2005   New diet soft drink Coca-Cola Zero is rolled out across the United States.

2007   Grand Opening of the new World of Coca-Cola in Atlanta, Georgia, a museum and retail attraction celebrating the Coca-Cola brand experience around the world.

As part of The Coca-Cola Company's Live Positively platform for sustainability, Coca-Cola Brazil and its bottling partners launched the "Brazilian Rainforest Water Program" in 2007 to support climate and watershed protection through the reforestation of Brazil's vital Atlantic Rainforest—an effort that serves to rehabilitate the environment, protect biodiversity, and restore ecosystem benefits once provided by the area.

2008

The 2008 Olympic Games in Beijing, China, open, marking the 80th year the Company has been associated with the Games. WE8 designer aluminum bottles are launched.

The Company announces a long-term target to recycle or re-use 100% of the aluminum beverage cans it sells in the United States. This new objective builds on the Company's previously announced goal to recycle or re-use 100% of its PET plastic bottles. Coca-Cola currently uses an average 60% recycled aluminum in its beverage cans.

2009

World's largest bottle-to-bottle recycling plant opens, launching "Give It Back," a multi-million-dollar marketing effort in support of recycling.

Plant Bottle™ is introduced, 100% recyclable and made from up to 30% plant-based material. It wins the DuPont award for packaging innovation.

The Coca-Cola Freestyle Vending Machine offers 106 individual drink choices, including add-in flavors. It eliminates 30 percent of water and packaging from the supply chain, reducing the system's total carbon footprint. The cartridges are also manufactured in a LEED-certified facility.

"Open Happiness" campaign launches. Open Happiness is an evolution of the Coke Side of Life, a campaign that featured award-winning commercials such as "Video Game," "Happiness Factory," and "It's Mine" and was used as the primary marketing platform in nearly every one of the more than 200 countries around the world where Coca-Cola is sold. The new campaign will continue to invite people to bring positivity, optimism and fun into their lives through engaging creative and an updated message.

2010   The 111 Navy Chair® is introduced. It is a PET version of the original Navy Chair produced by Emeco since the 1940s. Each chair contains 111 recycled plastic (PET) bottles diverted from landfills. The chair made its international debut at the Salone Internazionale del Mobile (Milan Furniture Fair) in Milan in May of 2010.

Coca-Cola announces "5 By 20", an ambitious goal to empower women entrepreneurs across the world. The Coca-Cola Company pledged to empower 5 million women entrepreneurs throughout Coca-Cola's global business system by 2020. The Coca-Cola Company made a commitment to grow the Company's Micro Distribution Centers in Africa. MDCs are an independent network of entrepreneurs who distribute Coca-Cola's beverage products to retailers, often by bicycle or pushcart. At the Clinton Global Initiative, the Company committed that 50% of all new MDCs would be run by women. The Company is well on track to achieve both targets as part of its commitments to the UN Millennium Development Goals.

ACKNOWLEDGMENTS

Acknowledgment and gratitude go to the hundreds of thousands of Coca-Cola System employees who have built the business over the past 125 years, and to the billions of consumers around the world who have made the Coca-Cola brand what it is today.

In particular, we would like to acknowledge the following professionals: *Assouline*: Martine Assouline, Prosper Assouline, Maya Camin, Eduard De Lange, Camille Dubois, Gina Amorelli, Jihyun Kim, Kristen Elizabeth Knapp, Esther Kremer, Nicole Lanctot, Naomi Liebowitz, Robert S. Mitchell, Mimi Crume Sterling; *Diecigroup*: Joseph Peter; *Deviant Ventures*: Umut Ozaydinli; *Exposure UK*: Zarah Leaman; *Gracie Films*: Denise Sirkot; *Definition 6*: Blakely Blalock; *L.A.C. Retouching*: Luc Alexis Chasleries; *Litchfield Entertainment Co., Inc.*: Ivy Tombak; *McCann Erickson*: Ahmed Fayez, Janet Regan, Heather Higgins; *Momentum*; *Mother London*; *Nexus Productions*: Cedric Gairard, Julia Parfitt; *OPUS*: Yu Tsai, 88 Phases, Bobby Heller, Opus Photo; *Psyop*: Kylie Matulick, Todd Mueller, Justin Booth-Clibborn, Adam Coffia; *TAG New York*: Ian Weed, Erin Hiers, Steven Miller; *Tiger Spike*: Luke Janssen, Matthew Turnbull; *Wieden + Kennedy*: Andrew Kay, Ryan Peterson, Amber Lavender, Teresa Lutz, Karen Crossley, Ilkay Dibekoglu, Courtney Trull, Brian Mead; *30 Point*: Adam Levy.

© 2011 Assouline Publishing
601 West 26th Street, 18th floor
New York, NY 10001, USA
Tel.: 212 989-6810   Fax: 212 647-0005

www.assouline.com

ISBN: 9782 75940 5145

Printed by Grafiche Milani S.p.a. (Italy).

CREDITS